nature doodles

LAND ART

OUTDOOR
MEDITATIVE FUN
for all ages

artist
DEANNA
WASHINGTON

I PLAY WITH STICKS.

Some people climb mountains, or make hats.
I play with sticks and stones.

Why? I was recently asked.

Go for a walk, and the monkey mind rides on your shoulder jabbering away the whole time. But pick up a stone and balance it on a stick and the brain flutters away. Silence.

Slide a bead onto a weed
Press a berry into a tree trunk
Slather a branch with blackberry juice
Poke a stone into a crevice
Hang a flower from the wrong tree
Align stones on a branch
Surround a puddle with petals
Paint stripes on a limb

Meditation—
to focus one's mind for a period of time, in silence, as a method of relaxation.

Tie
Weave
Arrange
Dangle
Stack
Bind
Connect

Why?
To behold nature in a different way
To create something and let it go
To express, unattached
To give freely
To bring a smile to my face and to the faces of others
To invite others to join me

Nature is our playground
It is our art store
Every stone as media
Every stick as decor
Every smile as reward.

—Deanna Washington
 January 2021

©2022 Deanna Washington

No part of this publication may be reproduced, distributed, or transmitted in any form or by any means, including photocopying, recording, or other electronic or mechanical methods, without the written permission of Deanna Washington, except for brief quotations embodied in critical reviews and certain other non-commercial uses permitted by copyright law.

www.DeannaWashington.com

DEDICATED TO BRISBANE, CA, COMMUNITY

You have embraced nature doodles with kind enthusiasm.

To those who participated in the "Stick Library." To all of you who have caught me in action on the trail and paused to chat with me. Many of these installations were done during covid so we had our masks on—I feel terrible that I don't recognize you all, but I super appreciate your enthusiasm.

To you who added jewelry and chimes, shells and holey stones to my doodles, and to any and all of you who made your own.

To the new friends I made on the trail—Arild, Jon and Shanna, Beth, Deborah, Laurie (and their husbands), to name a few. And to the dozens of people who stopped and talked to me, I apologize I don't remember names but every conversation lit up my day.

I cannot take credit for every doodle on Crocker Park Trail. Every time I see a new one that I did not make, I do a happy dance.

It's my heart's desire to show others how to look at and participate with nature in a new, fun, and personal way. Thank you, Brisbane for being a willing student.

What are land art and nature doodles?

I began my adventures with land art in January 2021. If you have never heard of land art, or environment art, look up Andy Goldsworthy — he's the granddaddy and gold star of the genre. His installations are large, involved, and time consuming, which is why I call my land art "nature doodles." They are just little doodles. Many of them take maybe 15 minutes, and none over two hours.

The materials I use are mostly from the 2.5 mile Crocker Park Trail in my town where I walk. This is the location of all but a few doodles that magically pop up when the spirit pulls me. Two larger installations, pages 72-75, decorated one of Brisbane's community parks.

Where do I get my ideas?

I follow environmental and land artists on social media. Some things, like the ladders (pages 26-29) and flower mandalas (pages 12-13), many people make. Other designs, such as the eucalyptus chain on page 50, I see ideas (a 3-leaf chain) that bounce me to other ideas (three 7-feet chains to hang in the trees).

Some of my more original ideas include the leaf-wrapped stone (page 69), and I've never seen anyone else make tree necklaces nor paint and string seeds.

Still other doodles, such as poking things where they don't belong, spring straight from my mischievous spirit. They likely aren't the most seen of my doodles, but they make me giggle when I make them. Imagine your mother says to clean your room, and she comes back in to find your area rug draped over the curtain rod, your books neatly stacked on the window sill, your clothes hanging from the fan...I delight in the unexpected.

WHY DO I NATURE DOODLE?

I considered sharing with you in depth several high-brow reasons for and benefits of nature doodling:

> MIND: Fresh air and movement reduces stress-inducing cortisol, the bad stuff, while increasing calming serotonin, the good stuff.
>
> BODY: Current research touts the physical benefits of an ambling nature walk over a power-walk, particularly for those of us over a certain age.
>
> SPIRIT: Nature bathing is trending—getting out into nature and use all your senses to reconnect with your soul and higher power.

But to be honest, I started for one simple reason: I hate the gray days of winter. To face something I don't enjoy, my way is to turn it into a game. For me, nature doodling became my way to get my bum outside and moving.

So while this could be a manual on meditation or how to nature doodle, I'm leaving it as a simple photobook and invite you to take my ideas, expand upon them and then embrace and express your own out in your local slice of nature.

I'll say it again: Go do some of your own. Say you're on your walk. What if you take 10 minutes to look around and imagine what you can stack or pile or arrange or thread or weave? For some of you this is natural; for others, it's just as mind-expanding as learning a new app would be for me.

Here in my 60th year, front and center of my attention is how mind expansion is as important to the brain as exercising is for the body. Just as making music fires so many parts of the brain, being outside in nature, creating, being silly, and laughing with your efforts orchestrates a soothing symphony of neuronal firing.

HOW TO USE THIS BOOK
First off, this is a documentation of the installations I created between January 2021-November 2022.

But that's mostly for me. Better yet for you, it's a challenge, and I hope an inspiration, for you to walk out your door, pick up sticks, and play.

I've arranged the book into four sections starting with the most basic—which include nearly half of the 130 nature doodles represented in the entire book—then moving to sections that require materials and perhaps more time.

Three Rules for Nature Doodling:
    1. Let go of perfection
    2. Have fun
    2.5. Let yourself be silly and imaginative
    3. Let it go

One of the most freeing things about nature doodling is this last step: let it go. "What do I do with it/where do I put it" becomes a central problem for a prolific artist. The heart on page 31 reached 6 feet in width and the swirl of stones on page 11 spanned a good 10 feet.

Letting it go also means being curious, rather than anxious, about how long each art piece survives. Some last hours or days. Others last months. The heart on page 41 is the oldest, fully intact doodle on the trail, installed nearly 2 years ago.

"It's a dangerous business, Frodo, going out your door. You step onto the road, and if you don't keep your feet, there's no knowing where you might be swept off to."
—J.R.R. Tolkien, The Lord of the Rings

THREE PHASES OF NATURE DOODLING

1. THE DOING

Sometimes I head out with nothing in mind and just see what shows up. Other times I plan ahead—perhaps with an idea that crept in as I drifted off to sleep the night before. The doing is surprisingly satisfying, even just balancing a line of stones on a limb. This phase can be enough. But wait, there is more!

2. THE PHOTOGRAPHING

Some photos, such as the mandalas on pages 12-13, look lovely viewed from straight down. But the right angle and amazing lighting can transform the photo into art unto itself.

Also, when the nature doodles are small or off to the side of the trail they can be hardly noticeable. Then the art becomes the photograph. I peer at the installation through my iphone from every angle seeing how the light changes and emphasizes the elements.

Other times, it's disappointing to find that the location or form make it near impossible to photograph well—the camera doesn't capture the doodles' cool essence because of the background or their gangly nature. Clearly I'm not always thinking of phase 2 when I'm motivated by phase 1.

Phase 2 is important for phase 3.

3. THE SHARING

Your initial audience in creating the nature doodle was yourself—for your joy and satisfaction. The next audience are the people who walk by and get a grin on their face. You don't get to see that audience. However, it's with sharing on social media that your piece becomes immortal and you get that extra dopamine hit of joy to hear people's reactions and feedback. *(See the sidebar on the bottom left of this page to see the power of sharing.)*

My favorite reaction of all is "This makes me smile." I see my mission as being a spreader of joy and smiles.

If you doubt the power of sharing, take a look at this photo.

This is what I saw on social media one random day that sent me down the rabbit hole to learn about land art and then to my own joy of creating it.

Drawings are created by Raking Leaves by Nikola Faller / Croatia /in Osijek city
facebook.com/slama.land.art3

Speaking of sharing, I would love to see the nature doodles you create! Tag me @dea_creatrix on instagram, pop me a photo and a note on my website DeannaWashington.com.

I'd love to hear about how this book inspires you to go outside and play with sticks and stones while your brain fires off a symphony of ideas and serotonin.

Nature Materials
Sticks
Stones
Leaves
Branches
Bark
Berries
Flowers
Fruit
Various plant parts
Other Materials
Twine/string/yarn (most used material—in a third of the doodles)
Wood beads
Cotton beads
Glue
Paint Staples
Posca paint pens
Natural clay
Polymer Clay
Crepe paper
Googly eyes
Tools
Clippers (most used tool—in a third of the doodles)
Hole punch
Leather gloves
Needle

TABLE OF CONTENTS

SECTION 1: Walk out the door...with empty pockets
mislay leaves 8
align stones 10
compose a mandala 12
organize berries 14
be mischievous 16
displace things 18
tie branches 20
dangle stuff 22
stack sticks 24
form ladders 26
shape hearts and faces 30
arrange flowers 32
weave 34

ok, sometimes with clippers

SECTION 2: Walk out the door...with a thing or two
twine 36
glue 46
staples 48
twine and a needle 50
twine and a hole punch 52
paint 54
paint pens and a hole punch 58
other materials 62

SECTION 3: Walk out the door...with preprepared materials
with prepared materials 66

SECTION 4: special events
celebrating days 72
community 80
honoring 98

Acknowledgments 90

SECTION 1:

WALK OUT THE DOOR WITH
NOTHING IN YOUR POCKETS

Walk out the door... and mislay leaves 9

Leaves

10   *Walk out the door...and align stones*

Walk out the door...and align stones 11

Stones

12   *Walk out the door...and compose a mandala*

Walk out the door...and compose a mandala 13

Stones, berries, leaves, sticks, seed pods, moss

14 *Walk out the door...and organize berries*

Berries

Walk out the door...and organize berries 15

16 *Walk out the door...and be mischievous*

Lavender, rosemary, eucalyptus branch,
poked in pampas grass

Walk out the door...and be mischievous 17

Blackberry juice dots;
stones balanced in a tree

18 *Walk out the door...and displace things*

Seed pods stuck on dead tree twigs;
eucalyptus bark inserted sideways;
assorted nonsense

Walk out the door...and displace things 19

Prickles stuck into tree crevices

20 *Walk out the door...and tie branches*

Walk out the door...and tie branches 21

Pampas grass ties

22 *Walk out the door...and dangle stuff*

Assorted plants hanging by pampas grass

Walk out the door...and dangle stuff   23

Sticks

Walk out the door...and stack sticks 25

26 *Walk out the door…and form ladders*

Walk out the door... and form ladders   27

Twigs

28   *Walk out the door...and form ladders*

Twigs

Walk out the door...and form ladders   29

30 *Walk out the door...and shape hearts or faces*

Sticks and stones

Walk out the door...and shape hearts or faces 31

32 *Walk out the door…and arrange flowers*

Flowers

Walk out the door...and arrange flowers 33

34   *Walk out the door...and weave*

Pampas grass

Walk out the door...and weave 35

SECTION 2:

WALK OUT THE DOOR WITH
A FEW THINGS IN YOUR POCKETS

Walk out the door...with twine   37

Dangle, tie and bind with twine

38 *Walk out the door...with twine*

Dangle, tie and bind with twine

Walk out the door... with twine   39

40   *Walk out the door...with twine*

Walk out the door...with twine   41

Weave and arrange with twine

42   *Walk out the door...with twine*

Walk out the door...with twine 43

Tie, shape, and bind with twine

44 *Walk out the door...with twine*

Walk out the door...with twine

Wrap, pull together and display with twine

46 *Walk out the door...with glue*

What won't be bound with twine can stick with glue

Walk out the door...with glue and twine   47

Walk out the door...with staples

Stapled leaves

Walk out the door...with staples 49

50   *Walk out the door...with twine and a needle*

Walk out the door...with twine and a needle 51

Threaded together

52 *Walk out the door...with twine and a hole punch*

Hole punch and hung,
with or without twine

Walk out the door... with twine and a hole punch   53

54   *Walk out the door...with paint*

I paint dead things

Walk out the door...with paint   55

56 *Walk out the door…with paint*

Walk out the door...with paint 57

Bring dead twigs, seeds, bark
to life with paint

58 *Walk out the door...with paint pens and a hole punch*

Hanging affirmations

Walk out the door…with paint pens and a hole punch   59

60   *Walk out the door...with paint pens and a hole punch*

Joy on a prickle bush;
faces on
trimmed branches

Walk out the door...with paint pens   61

62 *Walk out the door...with other materials*

Dried flowers tied onto fennel sticks;
painted 1-inch wooden beads poked onto fennel sticks

Walk out the door...with other materials 63

Painted 1/2 inch wooden beads poked onto fennel twigs

64 *Walk out the door...with other materials*

Paper-punched leaves strung onto bamboo steaks

Walk out the door...with other materials   65

One-inch cotton felt balls painted and poked onto twigs

SECTION 3:

WALK OUT THE DOOR WITH
PREPARED MATERIALS

Painted, drilled, strung, and hung seeds

Walk out the door...with prepared materials   67

Walk out the door...with prepared materials

Air-dry clay balls pressed into a tree, replicating the similar-shaped randomly placed fungus

Walk out the door...with prepared materials 69

Heart-shaped paper punched eucalyptus leaves,
glued to a large stone, nestled into a tree

70 *Walk out the door...with prepared materials*

Crepe paper flowers

Painted polymer clay butterflies

Walk out the door...with prepared materials 71

Polymer clay baked into sticks

SECTION 4:

WALK OUT THE DOOR FOR
SPECIAL EVENTS

New Year's Day Field of Strength

Walk out the door...celebrating 73

PHOTO: KEVIN FRYER

74   *Walk out the door...celebrating*

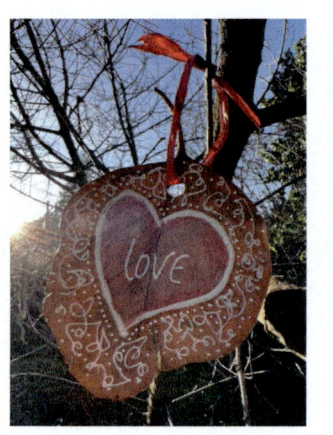

Valentine's Day Garden of Love

Walk out the door...celebrating 75

Pride, 2022
Yarn on tree branch

Walk out the door...celebrating 77

19 sets of googly eyes for Halloween

78 *Walk out the door...celebrating*

Happy Anniversary, hunny

Walk out the door...celebrating   79

For my 60th birthday, I wound and hung 60 of these circles—representing hugs

I invited fellow walkers to participate in a "stick library."
- Take a stick
- Paint it
- Return it
- Exchange it with one you enjoy

Over 20 people took sticks and brought them back. I have no idea who they are, and I fear I did not get photos of absolutely all of them.

Here, however, is the lion's share. The creativity blew my mind.

Thank you—you know who you are!

Walk out the door...with community   81

82 *Walk out the door...with community*

Walk out the door...with community 83

84 *Walk out the door...with community*

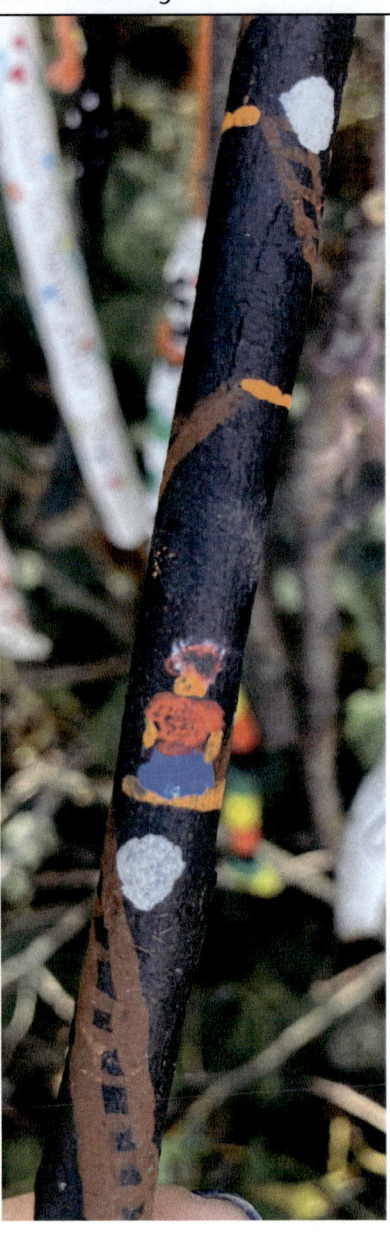

Walk out the door...with community 85

86 *Walk out the door...with community*

Walk out the door...with community 87

Walk out the door...in honor

Created in honor of Ukraine the week the war began

Walk out the door...in honor   89

RIP nephew Benny. My sister Arline's special-needs son, age 38, passed away in July 2022. I left the house knowing I was going create something in honor of him, and this is what begged to be made. He loved all things Native American

ACKNOWLEDGMENTS

First of all, thank you to Cindy Brehmer. When I asked "Wanna do a thing?" she said yes without even asking what we'd be doing. We made my (our) first naturedoodle (eucalyptus leaf mandala on page 13). Then she happily helped with several more.

Thank you to Theresa Jimendez, creative whiz, made these sweet doodles on the page to the right that were included in several installations. Theresa brought her friend, Zoe Heimdal, to help me assemble the Garden of Love. They both created gorgeous decorated leaves and hangy things to include.

Gratitude to Kevin Fryer, who photographed many of the pieces and then asked for a tour of the doodles when approximately 60 were on the 2.5 mile trail. He helped with the installation of The Field of Strength and photographed leaves. His husband, Sisto Flores (pictured here "eating"), filmed the process and made a video that can be seen on my website, DeannaWashington.com.

Thank you to the other doodle helpers, Leesa Whitten Greenlee, Anna Lynch, and Joshua Washington. Thank you to Lia Griffith, my sister, for her crepe paper flower pattern and materials, page 70.

And finally, thank you to Lise Dumont for reading over this book and editing it for a better read.

Walk out the door...with acknowledgments 91

About the artist/photographer/author

Deanna Washington's career as a graphic designer morphed during covid to creating outdoor public art and land art. In 2021 she published *Peace Pickets: Picket Ladies and Remembering What Connects Us.*

She has self-published a half-dozen non-fiction books and is currently writing her first novel about Peter Pan's sister, her muse, who also doesn't want to grow up.

Her husband, Curtis, retired from his high school physics teaching career and is known around town as "Deanna's husband."

Made in the USA
Middletown, DE
16 November 2024